FR. MARK TOUPS

Rejoice!

Advent Meditations
with Joseph

ASCENSION

West Chester, Pennsylvania

Nihil obstat: Reverend Samuel Brice Higginbotham
                  Censor Librorum
                  August 15, 2019

Imprimatur: +Most Reverend Shelton J. Fabre
                  Bishop of Houma-Thibodaux
                  August 15, 2019

Ascension
Post Office Box 1990
West Chester, PA 19380
1-800-376-0520
ascensionpress.com

Cover art: Mike Moyers (*Onward to Bethlehem* © 2019 Mike Moyers, Franklin, TN)
Interior art: Mike Moyers (*Joseph the Carpenter, The Angel Visits Joseph, Embarking for Bethlehem, No Room, Shine* © 2019 Mike Moyers, Franklin, TN)
Printed in the United States of America
ISBN 978-1-945179-99-0

CONTENTS

HOW TO USE THIS JOURNAL

Daily Meditations

This journal you have in your hands is an Advent prayer journal with daily meditations. Each week of *Rejoice!* has a theme that allows you to dive deeply into the lessons Joseph has to share about welcoming Jesus into his life. Each week's theme will help you walk closer and closer to the ultimate goal of preparing for the person of Jesus, not just preparing for the day of Christmas.

Since the fourth week of Advent can vary in length, we have provided seven meditations. So, whether the week is two days long or seven, you will have enough content for each day of the season.

Community

Community is a key component in the journey to holiness. Advent provides a wonderful opportunity to take a little more time to focus on your prayer and grow stronger in friendships on the shared journey to heaven.

The ideal is for a whole parish to take up *Rejoice!* and journey together as a community. You can learn more about how to provide *Rejoice!* to a large parish group at **rejoiceprogram.com,** with information about bulk discounts and parish mission nights with the *Rejoice!* videos.

If you are unable to experience *Rejoice!* as a whole parish, consider a small group setting. Use *Rejoice!* as a family devotion for Advent or get together with a few friends to discuss your prayer and how God is speaking to you in this season.

This doesn't mean you can't use *Rejoice!* as an individual. You can take this journey with Joseph through Advent even if you are not meeting in a group or talking about it with friends. You are still not alone – Catholics all over the country are on the same journey you are. This journal is a place for you to speak to God and to hear and see all that he has to show you.

Videos

To accompany the journal, *Rejoice!* offers videos with Father Mark Toups, Sister Miriam James Heidland, and Father Josh Johnson. Through their witness, conversation, and prayer, you will find fresh insights into the details of Joseph's life and his preparation to welcome Jesus.

The program includes a primary *Rejoice!* video and thematic weekly videos. Each Sunday of Advent, you will get access to a quick video to energize your reflections and encourage you in your prayer each week. Sign up for these weekly videos at **rejoiceprogram.com** to receive them by email.

FOR YOUR PRAYER

Imaginative Prayer

Each day's reflection will end with a prompt titled "For Your Prayer." There, you will be given a Scripture passage to read, and a short prayer to pray with. Here is how to pray with these Scripture passages.

Prepare

Open your Bible, and read the passage once. Get familiar with the words. Then slowly read the passage a second time. Pay attention to how you feel as you read. Pay attention to which words strike you.

Next, use your imagination to pray with the passage. In his book *Meditation and Contemplation,* Rev. Tim Gallagher, O.M.V., writes, "In this manner of praying, Saint Ignatius tells us, we imaginatively see the persons in the Bible passage, we hear the words they speak, and we observe the actions they accomplish in the event." So, jump into the Scripture passage. Be in the scene with Mary. Once the scene comes to its natural conclusion, continue with A.R.R.R.

A.R.R.R.

A.R.R.R. is the next step in imaginative prayer. It stands for Acknowledge, Relate, Receive, Respond.

You have sat with God's word. You have entered into the scene. Now, once you feel God is saying something to you, *acknowledge* what stirs within you. Pay attention to your thoughts, feelings, and desires. These are important.

After you have acknowledged what's going on inside your heart, *relate* that to God. Don't just think about your thoughts, feelings, and desires. Don't just think about God or how God might react. Relate to God. Tell him how you feel. Tell him what you think. Tell him what you want. Share all your thoughts, feelings, and desires with God. Share everything with him.

Once you have shared everything with God, *receive.* Listen to what he's telling you. It could be a subtle voice you hear. It could be a memory that pops up. Maybe he invites you to re-read the Scripture passage. Perhaps he invites you into a still, restful silence. Trust that God is listening to you, and receive what he wants to share with you.

Now, *respond.* Your response could be more conversation with God. It could be a resolution. It could be tears or laughter. Respond to what you're receiving.

Finally, after picturing the scene with Joseph and acknowledging, relating, receiving, and responding, the last step is *journal.* Keep a record this Advent of what your prayer was like. It doesn't have to be lengthy. It could be a single word, a sentence or two about what God told you, or how the day's reflection struck you. Regardless of how you do it, journaling will help you walk with Joseph this Advent. We have provided space in this journal each day for you.

Plan Your Prayer Time with the Five W's

Advent can be a busy season. As you dedicate yourself to prayer this Advent, there is no better safeguard than a good plan. Fr. Josh Johnson, one of the presenters in the *Rejoice!* videos, recommends the Five W's as a method of planning. Here's how it works. Every Sunday, look at your calendar and write out your plan for each of the next six days, answering the following questions: When? Where? What? Who? and Why?

WHEN will I spend time with Jesus?

WHERE will I spend time with Jesus?

WHAT are Jesus and I going to do together?

WHO will hold me accountable to my time with Jesus?

WHY am I prioritizing my time with Jesus?

Having a plan will help you walk with Joseph using *Rejoice!* this Advent.

Nazareth

WHO IS JOSEPH?

What kind of person was he?

I regret that, for most of my life, I thought of Joseph through a skewed imagination. I wrongly interpreted the first chapter of Matthew. I grew up assuming that the angel was sent by God to convince Joseph to marry Mary. I eventually came to see how Matthew 1 is much more about Joseph's holiness than it is about God sending an angel to "convince" him of anything. Over time, I have come to understand that Joseph is not a passive man holding a flower, nor is he someone who needed to be persuaded to follow God's plan.

When I was growing up, every image I saw of Joseph was of him holding a white lily. My father taught me that Joseph was a carpenter, and I spent hundreds of hours as a kid with my dad doing carpentry work. When my dad was remodeling our house and working just as Joseph did, he did not look like a "flowery" St. Joseph. Men who work hard by the sweat of their brows do not look like Joseph with a flower. I am saddened that so many have this image of St. Joseph—an image which does not capture the strength of this great saint.

A dear friend of mine helped me greatly when he said, "Artists are right in what they affirm, and wrong in what they deny." There is a truth about Joseph that artists convey when they depict him holding a lily; however, this image is incomplete. St. Joseph invites us to learn more about the reality of who he is.

Joseph was a *man*. He was chosen by God for one of the most important tasks in the history of the world. Imagine for a moment what it would be like for a woman of Mary's purity to invite you into her heart, *only to expect that same depth of purity from you once you were there*. Joseph would have needed heroic courage to stay committed to virtue to love Mary on *her terms*. Imagine for a moment what it would be like to protect Jesus as a child. Imagine for a moment what it would be like to kneel at the bedside of a six-year-old Jesus, knowing that God chose *you* to teach Jesus how to pray.

So, who is Joseph? What kind of person was he?

Welcome to the first week of Advent, where we will begin to come to know who Joseph *really* was.

For Your Prayer

"Joseph, son of David, do not be afraid to take Mary as your wife, for the child conceived in her is from the Holy Spirit. She will bear a son, and you are to name him Jesus, for he will save his people from their sins."
– Matthew 1:20-21

WHERE

> **"Be still, and know**
>
> **that I am God."**

—Psalm 46:10

AT THE TIME

of Jesus, Nazareth was a tiny village in the hills, twelve miles southwest of the Sea of Galilee. It was a small community of approximately two hundred families, steeped in traditional Jewish culture in a world that had been radically influenced by Greek thought. With a total population of fewer than five hundred people, it is easy to believe that everyone knew everyone—and that everyone knew everything about everyone. Nazareth was small. It was quiet. It was unimportant in the eyes of the Romans, and it was inconsequential in the minds of most Jews at the time.

Nazareth was where Joseph lived. We can imagine that the exterior realities of this small village helped shape his interior reality. Nazareth's simplicity nurtured the singular focus of Joseph's life: God. The humble poverty of Nazareth fostered the virtue of humility within Joseph's heart. Its slow pace cultivated the contemplative rhythm of Joseph's life. Nazareth was more than where Joseph lived; it was where he *was*. He was content with *where* he was because he was content with *who* he was.

It is important for us to consider Nazareth, with all of its simplicities and imperfections, as the home God chose for Joseph. Why? Because many of us also find ourselves in imperfect families, imperfect seasons of life, and imperfect situations. Let us begin the journey by asking: How do you feel about *where* you are in life? Your life … your marriage … your vocation … your family … your health … your job … your past … your dreams? How do you feel about where you are in life?

The temptation whispers like this: "If I were there and not here, then I'd be happy … If I had another job, then I would be happy … If I could just be somewhere else or with someone else, then

I would be happy ..." I would reverently invite all of us to consider that, while our current circumstances are important and should be honored, it is more important to start with where God is. If God has led us to where we are, then our happiness will not come from the *place* we are; it will come from God. God was in Nazareth because that is where Joseph was. God is with you; he is where you are.

Where do you want to be by the end of Advent? What do you desire from the Lord from now to Christmas? If God could do anything in your life during this season of Advent, what would you want the Lord to do?

For Your Prayer

Joseph prayed with the Psalms. Begin by slowly reading Psalm 46, especially verse 10. Read it a few times. Consider how often Joseph prayed with these Old Testament verses. What is God saying to you in the Bible passage? How does it apply to your life? What do you want to say to God?

"Father, I beg you to make this Advent my best ever. Help me to slow down, embrace the quiet, and to find you with me, no matter where I am."

What words stood out to you as you prayed?
What did you find stirring in your heart?

_____

_____

_____

_____

_____

_____

_____

_____

_____

_____

_____

_____

_____

_____

_____

_____

_____

_____

_____

First Week — SUNDAY

CHOSEN

"My soul clings to you; your
right hand upholds me."

—Psalm 63:8

WHO IS JOSEPH?

What kind of person was he? Over time, I have come to understand that Joseph was not the passive man depicted holding a white lily, nor is he someone who needed to be convinced of God's plan. What sparked my quest to more fully understand Joseph?

While searching for something unrelated in the *Catechism of the Catholic Church*, I came across paragraph 239, which speaks of God's fatherhood. I read how the image of God as Father "emphasizes God's immanence, the intimacy between Creator and creature. The language of faith thus draws on the human experience of parents, who are in a way the first representatives of God for man. But this experience also tells us that human parents are fallible and can disfigure the face of fatherhood and motherhood."

It hit me like a ton of bricks: Parents are "the first representatives of God for man." That means God intentionally *chose* one man— *one man* in all of human history—to "represent" fatherhood to Jesus. This was Joseph. When God the Father wanted to show the child Jesus what human fatherhood looked like, he chose Joseph. In choosing Joseph, God was careful to choose a man who would not "disfigure the face of fatherhood" on God's behalf. Joseph, then, is more than a white lily; he was a man of profound holiness. He was a man of authentic masculinity. He embodied virtue. He lived quietly "on the inside." He had a mature interior life and understood obedience as that which fosters intimacy and receptivity with God. He loved the Word of God. *He loved God.* All of this helps us appreciate how Joseph was chosen to image authentic fatherhood to Jesus. ——————————————

God has also chosen *you*. You have been chosen by God to be his representative. Certainly, if you are a parent, the Church reminds you that parents "are in a way the first representatives of God for man." However, your baptism means that you have been *chosen* to be God's witness to the world: at work, in your family, and in your community. God chose *you*. Our lives reveal something. We are already setting an example. By the way we live our lives, we set an example for our spouse, our children, our friends, our colleagues, other Christians, and everyone we meet. We are already setting an example. The question is what type of an example are we setting? What do you want your life to reveal?

Our Advent story peaks with Christmas, which reveals God's desire for us. God wants your holiness. So, if God could do anything in your life, what would you want?

For Your Prayer

Joseph prayed with the Psalms. Begin by slowly reading Psalm 63. Read it a few times. Consider how often Joseph prayed with these Old Testament verses. What is God saying to you in the Bible passage? How does it apply to your life? What do you want to say to God?

"Father, I beg you to make this Advent my best ever. Help me to slow down so that I can find you with me. I want to be the person you have called me to be. I want to be an example."

What words stood out to you as you prayed?
What did you find stirring in your heart?

_____

_____

_____

_____

_____

_____

_____

_____

_____

_____

_____

_____

_____

_____

_____

_____

_____

_____

_____

_____

_____

JUST

> ❝ In all that
> he does,
> he prospers. ❞
>
> —Psalm 1:3

THE SCRIPTURES

tell us much less about Joseph than they tell about Mary. However, what the Scriptures do say is significant. In Matthew 1:19 we read, "her husband Joseph, being a just man…" What is a "just" man? Why is this significant?

As Pope Benedict XVI writes, "The Old Testament idea of a whole life lived according to Sacred Scripture is summed up in the idea of 'a just man.'"[1] To understand Joseph as "just" we understand that his "whole life lived according to Sacred Scripture." *All* of Joseph was available to God. The Pope continues, "Psalm 1 presents the classic image of the 'just' man. We might well think of it as a portrait of the spiritual figure of St. Joseph. A just man, it tells us, is one who maintains living contact with the word of God ... He is like a tree, planted beside the flowing waters ... The flowing waters, from which he draws nourishment, naturally refer to the living word of God."[2]

Why was Joseph "just"? Because he lived his "whole life lived according to Sacred Scripture." He maintained "living contact with the word of God, who 'delights in the law of the Lord.'"

You have heard it said: "You are what you eat." Our bodies become what we put into them. Likewise, intellectually and spiritually, "You are what you 'eat.'" What we consume interiorly is what we become interiorly. Joseph was just because he maintained a steady diet of God's word. He longed for holiness; therefore, he was intentional about "consuming" holiness. Joseph maintained "living contact with the word of God." Imagine the hidden moments in Joseph's life. Early in the morning, before everyone else rises, Joseph makes time to meditate on God's word. During the day, while working, Joseph is considering the Scriptures that he read earlier that morning. Later that day, when he is finished a day's work, instead of "unplugging" and "vegging out" (as we do with television or the Internet), Joseph chooses to choose that which will make him healthy. At the end of the day, before he sleeps, he chooses Scripture as the last words on his mind before he falls asleep.

How is your spiritual diet? Where do you "go" when you are off and have free time? Where do you go when you have nothing else to do? Imagine what your life could look like if you lived more firmly rooted in God. By his example, Joseph taught Jesus how to choose to choose God. Imagine if he taught you the same. Would you like that? If so, can you ask for that?

For Your Prayer

Joseph prayed with the Psalms. Begin by slowly reading Psalm 1, especially verse 3. Read it a few times. Consider how often Joseph prayed with these Old Testament verses. What is God saying to you in the Bible passage? How does it apply to your life? What do you want to say to God?

"Father, I beg you to make this Advent my best ever. Help me to slow down and look deep within. Help to live in you."

**What words stood out to you as you prayed?
What did you find stirring in your heart?**

_____

_____

_____

_____

_____

_____

_____

_____

_____

_____

_____

_____

_____

_____

_____

_____

_____

_____

_____

_____

First Week — TUESDAY

PROTECTOR

Make me to know

" your ways, O LORD; "

teach me your paths.

—Psalm 25:4

A MAN OF GREAT

virtue, it was "to assure fatherly protection for Jesus that God chose Joseph to be Mary's spouse."[3] Joseph was chosen for *protection*. We see this most clearly illustrated in Matthew 2:13-14: "Behold, an angel of the Lord appeared to Joseph in a dream and said, 'Rise, take the child and his mother, and flee to Egypt … for Herod is about to search for the child, to destroy him.' And he rose and took the child and his mother by night and departed to Egypt."

Joseph protected his family in the face of danger. However, later we see a difference face of Joseph's protection—his sharp discernment: "But when Herod died, behold, an angel of the Lord appeared in a dream to Joseph in Egypt, saying, 'Rise, take the child and his mother, and go to the land of Israel, for those who sought the child's life are dead.' And he rose and took the child and his mother and went to the land of Israel." Now, notice what happens next: "But when he heard that Archelaus reigned over Judea in place of his father Herod, he was afraid to go there, and being warned in a dream he withdrew to the district of Galilee. And he went and dwelt in a city called Nazareth, that what was spoken by the prophets might be fulfilled, 'He shall be called a Nazarene'" (Matthew 2:19-23). Joseph's discernment took him to Nazareth rather than to danger.

Joseph also protected Mary's virginity with profound reverence. Pope Benedict XVI writes, "It follows that God, by giving Joseph to the Virgin, did not give him to her only as a companion for life, a witness of her virginity and protector of her honor."[4] While living completely his full identity as a husband, Joseph chose to love Mary within the fullness of God's plan for her. Joseph protected Mary's virginity by loving her as God would have him do. Joseph loved Mary *on her terms*, not his.

Joseph's protecting Mary's virginity actually revealed his strength. Strength is not always found in what you *can* do, but often in what you choose *not* to do. Authentic strength is not found in one's capacity to "do whatever you want" but in sometimes choosing *not* to do whatever you want. Holiness is tested by one's ability to restrain oneself *for the sake of holiness*, for if a man cannot say no, what does that say about his yes?

What is Joseph's lack of self-centeredness saying to you? What is his choice to live life by a different standard saying to you?

For Your Prayer

Joseph prayed with the Psalms. Begin by slowly reading Psalm 25:1–10. Read it a few times. Consider how often Joseph prayed with these Old Testament verses. What is God saying to you in the Bible passage? How does it apply to your life? What do you want to say to God?

"Father, I beg you to make this Advent my best ever. Help me to no longer live for myself, but to live for you and for others. Give me the courage to let go of me and live for you."

What words stood out to you as you prayed?
What did you find stirring in your heart?

_____

_____

_____

_____

_____

_____

_____

_____

_____

_____

_____

_____

_____

_____

_____

_____

_____

_____

_____

_____

_____

_____

OBEDIENT

" The Lord your God is with you wherever you go. "

—Joshua 1:9

JOSEPH'S WAS A MAN

of *obedience*. Matthew 1:20 reads: "Joseph, son of David, do not fear to take Mary your wife." Many speculate that he was afraid because he did not know what it meant that Mary conceived through the Holy Spirit. Perhaps he was afraid because he *did* understand. Perhaps his fear was because he felt unworthy. Joseph chooses God, even in the face of fear.

While describing the flight into Egypt, Matthew 2:14 tells us: "And he rose and took the child and his mother by night and departed to Egypt." He left by night, which means he left immediately. God said move and move now. Joseph was obedient. No debate; no questions. Once Joseph knew it was God speaking, his only response was "yes."

Luke chapter 2 also speaks of Joseph's obedience. The census was not in his plans, yet Joseph was obedient. Chapter 2 ends with both verses 40 and 52 mentioning Nazareth as the place where Jesus learns "wisdom." The word Greek word *sophia* literally means "the capacity to understand and act according to wisdom." To function according to wisdom is to be obedient.

Joseph only discerns the "what" so that he can discern the "who." Once Joseph knows it is the voice of God, his only response is "yes." He is obedient to a person, not merely to a task. We live at a time and in a culture where obedience is no longer considered a virtue. We are taught to "be your own person" and "live life on your own terms." How many times do we hear people say, "You only live once. Do whatever makes you happy." If we are to discover Advent through the eyes of Joseph, we must understand Joseph's obedience to a *person*—God. Joseph's obedience was *a response to a relationship*, not yielding to a task.

Imagine for a moment if you knew God so well that you wanted to be obedient just as Joseph was. Imagine if you heard God speak to you as Joseph heard God speak to him. Would your life, your marriage, your family, and your virtue be better or worse if you actually had that type of relationship with God? Now is the time to ask that question. What do you want? What is God saying to you?

For Your Prayer

Joseph prayed with the story of the Chosen People's entry into the Promised Land. Joseph would have known the story from the book of Joshua. Begin by slowly reading Joshua 1:1–10. Read it a few times. Consider how often Joseph prayed with these Old Testament verses. What is God saying to you in the Bible passage? How does it apply to your life? What do you want to say to God?

"Father, I beg you to make this Advent my best ever. Help me to no longer live for myself, but to live for you and for others. I beg for the grace to be as obedient to you as Joseph was."

**What words stood out to you as you prayed?
What did you find stirring in your heart?**

INTERIOR

"You will seek me
and find me; when
you seek me
with all your heart."

—Jeremiah 29:13

A MATURE INTERIOR

life requires intentionality. Silence is necessary for holiness. In fact, it is necessary for humanity. Pope Benedict XVI, while speaking on the importance of the interior life, said that many of us want "to fill every empty moment with music and images, out of fear of feeling this very emptiness. This is a trend that has always existed, especially among the young and in the more developed urban contexts but today it has reached a level such as to give rise to talk about anthropological mutation. Some people are no longer able to remain for long periods in silence and solitude."[5] Whew– "anthropological mutation." What does that mean? It means that when we grow less and less accustomed to silence, we become less human. Human beings need silence like the heart needs oxygen

A mature interior life also requires awareness, it presupposes that I am aware of what is happening *within*. St. Augustine speaks of the pattern that plagues modern man, as he writes: "Late have I loved you, Beauty so ancient and so new, late have I loved you! Lo, you were within, but I outside, seeking there for you, and upon the shapely things you have made I rushed headlong—I, misshapen. You were with me, but I was not with you. They held me back far from you, those things which would have no being, were they not in you."[6] God was "within" Augustine, yet his attention was in the external world. In fact, Augustine admits that, "You were with me, but I was not with you." We can easily deduce that Joseph was a man keenly aware of his interior life. Joseph lived *within*—there *with* God.

A mature interior life also requires prayer. Monsignor John Cippel reminded me once, "Prayer is a seesaw, not a swing." It only takes one person to swing, but it takes two people to seesaw. Prayer is an encounter with an Other, namely God. No doubt Joseph prayed not just daily but throughout the day. Because of his spiritual maturity, Joseph would have lived in a harmonious rhythm with God in prayer.

You would not be reading this journal unless you wanted more from God. Your commitment to learning more about Joseph reveals your desire for more. Consider Joseph's interior life—especially silence, awareness, and prayer. Spiritual growth *is* possible. *Your* spiritual growth is possible. Consider the three things above: silence, awareness, and prayer. Which one is God asking you to start with? Start with one and grow from there. Where is God calling you to commit: silence, awareness, or prayer?

For Your Prayer

Joseph prayed with words from the prophet Jeremiah. Begin by slowly reading Jeremiah 29:11–14. Read it a few times. Consider how often Joseph prayed with these Old Testament verses. What is God saying to you in the Bible passage? How does it apply to your life? What do you want to say to God?

"Father, I beg you to make this Advent my best ever. Help me to grow in my spiritual life. Teach me how to take the next step towards you."

What words stood out to you as you prayed? What did you find stirring in your heart?

_____

_____

_____

_____

_____

_____

_____

_____

_____

_____

_____

_____

_____

_____

_____

_____

_____

_____

IDENTITY

"Fear not, for I have
redeemed you;
I have called you by
name, you are mine."

—Isaiah 43:1

I AM CONVINCED

that there is a question looming in the heart of every man. In my experience as a man with countless hours of self-reflection, it is *the* question, one that has more of an influence on men than almost anything else in life. The question is: "Do I have what it takes to be a man?" Many men seek to answer this question from the utilitarian paradigm of "mission, identity, relationship." Most men believe that their identity is determined by what they *do*. Their mission, their *doing* or success, is often what drives them. From the mission they glean their identity, often living in the label they place upon themselves from the presence of, or lack of, success. Within this paradigm, their relationship with God is determined not by God, but by who they think they are and what they think they deserve.

What if there were another way to see the paradigm? The Institute for Priestly Formation has helped me understand the "mission, identity, relationship" trap and the truth of "relationship, identity, mission." Our relationship with God is always first and foremost. Nothing is more important than our relationship with God. From the relationship, we receive our identity. Our identity is *received*, not earned. From our God-given identity, we respond to our relationship with God as we receive the mission from him.

Joseph knew *who* he was because Joseph knew *whose* he was. What we know about Joseph, namely his marriage to Mary and his raising Jesus, are both given to him by God. However, God's first words to Joseph through the angel remind him of his identity. "Joseph, *son* of David, do not fear..." (Matthew 1:20, emphasis added). Joseph was a man who lived in the order and freedom of "relationship, identity, mission." Joseph's identity was determined by God and God alone. Joseph received his identity from God, and from there the rest of his life flowed.

How do you define who you are? How do you view yourself? Is your perception of your identity most influenced by God or what you do? If you are living under the weight of "mission, identity, relationship," imagine what life might feel like if you lived in the truth of "relationship, identity, mission." Imagine for a moment if you no longer had to prove who you are or work so hard to meet others' expectations. Imagine if God reordered your life so that you lived more like Joseph. Would you want that?

What has been the theme of this first week? Is there a theme of what he has been saying to you? Is there a pattern of what you want from God?

For Your Prayer

Joseph prayed with the Old Testament, especially the words from the prophet Isaiah. Begin by slowly reading Isaiah 43:1–7. Read it a few times. Consider how often Joseph prayed with these Old Testament verses. What is God saying to you in the Bible passage? How does it apply to your life? What do you want to say to God?

"Father, I beg you to make this Advent my best ever. Help me to know whose I am so I can know who I am."

What words stood out to you as you prayed? What did you find stirring in your heart?

First Week — SATURDAY

The Second Week of Advent

Galilee

AS MENTIONED

last week, I grew up with serious misunderstandings about Joseph. I wrongly interpreted the first chapter of Matthew, assuming that the angel had been sent by God to "convince" Joseph to marry Mary. Praise God, I later came to see how Matthew 1 is much more about Joseph's holiness than it is about God sending an angel to convince him of anything.

As we begin this second week of Advent, we enter into a distinct part of the Advent story *through the eyes of Joseph*. This week we shall unpack all that happened with Joseph and Mary's betrothal, the news of Mary's conception, the decision to divorce, and their surrender to God's plan. This sacred part of the story reveals holiness in Joseph that is important for us to understand how we can *see* Advent through his eyes.

It is easier to know some*thing* than it is to love some*one*. It is easier to *do* something than it is to *love* someone. To love the way that the Bible reveals how we are to love is the hardest thing that we will ever do. If we are to understand Advent *through the eyes of Joseph*, we must understand the reality of what was required of him as a husband. In fact, when I first developed the outline for this book, it was week three and the journey to Bethlehem that most excited me. Then, as I began writing, week two emerged as the most piercing and challenging reality that I have considered in a long time.

I want to invite you into Joseph's heart, his *real* heart. This week, Joseph invites you to make a pilgrimage through his interior life and the strength of purity that is required to marry the only sinless woman born outside the Garden. By way of invitation, this week's meditations may have more length, but their length is to meant to provide a larger canvas for what God is painting as the reality of Joseph's heart.

It is rare that someone invites you into the deepest recesses of their heart; however, Joseph himself is extending his hand to you now and inviting you to *really* get to know him.

Welcome to week two, *welcome to Joseph's heart.*

For Your Prayer

"Trust in the LORD with all your heart, and do not rely on your own insight; in all your ways acknowledge to him, and he will make straight your paths."
– Proverbs 3:5-6

LOVE

"He is like a

tree planted by

streams of water,

that yields its

fruit in its season."

—**Psalm 1:3**

WHAT DID IT MEAN

that Joseph was "betrothed" to Mary? *Redemptoris Custos,* an apostolic exhortation written by St. John Paul II, reads: "According to Jewish custom, marriage took place in two stages: first, the legal marriage was celebrated, and then, only after a certain period of time, the husband brought the wife into his own house. Thus, before he lived with Mary, Joseph was already her 'husband.'"[7] The Pope continues: "Mary, however, preserved her deep desire to give herself exclusively to God."[8]

What does it mean that Mary "preserved her deep desire to give herself exclusively to God"? Mary made a private vow of consecration to God prior to her betrothal and intended to maintain this consecration throughout her marriage to Joseph. During the Annunciation, "The Angel does not ask Mary to remain a virgin; it is Mary who freely reveals her intention of virginity. The choice of love that leads her to consecrate herself totally to the Lord by a life of virginity is found in this commitment."[9]

Joseph would have known about Mary's intended virginal consecration before, during, and after his decision to betroth her. Joseph's knowledge of Mary's consecration reveals much about his own heart.

St. Thomas Aquinas states: "To love is to will the good of another."[10] As Joseph loves Mary, he longs "to will the good" for her. *He only wants what is best for her.* He does not grasp at what he wants. He does not "take" from Mary. He lives with a posture of only wanting to receive Mary on *her* terms, not *his.* We should be careful to never project onto Joseph our secular inclinations. Joseph never thinks: "I deserve this" or "As a husband, I deserve that." Joseph loves Mary *with virtue.* Joseph accepts Mary's virginity because he protects her consecration. Joseph embraces Mary as *she is* because that is what true love is.

As we move through Joseph's heart, notice there is no grasping. There is no desire to take from Mary. I invite you to "feel" what you feel in his heart, as well as what you feel in *your* heart. To love well requires that we do not grasp or take from someone. To love purely requires that we allow the other person to reveal themselves to us in time, as they choose to do so. This requires the virtue of patience. As we stand together Joseph's heart, patience is the air we breathe. What stirs within you as you consider the purity of Joseph's love for Mary? Pause now. Pay attention. Listen to your heart. What is God saying to you?

For Your Prayer

Last week you prayed with Psalm 1. Return to Psalm 1 today. Imagine it as a description of Joseph. Consider the only way to love as Joseph loved is to live as Psalm 1 teaches.

"Father, I beg you to purify my heart. Teach me to love as Joseph loved."

What words stood out to you as you prayed?
What did you find stirring in your heart?

_____

_____

_____

_____

_____

_____

_____

_____

_____

_____

_____

_____

_____

_____

_____

_____

_____

_____

_____

_____

_____

AWE

"Present your
bodies as a living
sacrifice, holy
and acceptable
to God."

—Romans 12:1

JOSEPH WAS FULLY

aware of Mary's consecration to God, including the exclusive offering of her virginity. Therefore, it is essential that we understand his response to her "... found to be with child of the Holy Spirit" (Matthew 1:18). Many of us struggle with this part of the story for three reasons:

- First, it is difficult for many of us to imagine that Mary desired total consecration to God, while at the same time desiring to be married to Joseph. When we do this, we lower Mary to our standards.

- Second, it is difficult to believe that Mary and Joseph would have *freely chosen* to embrace abstinence. We may struggle because we cannot conceive how they had an intimate, full marriage while refraining from marital relations.

- Third, it is difficult for many of us to believe that Joseph actually believed Mary. Perhaps this is because of our particular interpretation of Matthew 1:20 or because of why we assume he chose to divorce her.

This book is a gift to "see" Advent through the eyes of Joseph. Let us remember that Joseph was a just man. Last week we read: "Psalm 1 presents the classic image of the 'just' man. ... A just man, it tells us, is one who maintains living contact with the word of God."[11] The just man lives in the word of God; therefore, as *just*, we can be confident that Joseph knew the Old Testament well.

Joseph would have known Isaiah 7:14: "Therefore, the Lord himself will give you a sign. Behold, a young woman shall conceive and bear a son, and shall call his name Immanuel." Isaiah's prophecy is about a *virginal* conception of the Messiah, and *Joseph knew this*. Tomorrow, we will unpack Matthew 1:19, which states "Joseph, being a just man and unwilling to put her to shame, resolved to send her away quietly." We will see how both St. Bernard of Clairvaux and St. Thomas Aquinas both contended that Joseph was acting out of profound reverence for his awe of what happened and not in disbelief of what Mary said or a belief of infidelity. Joseph was in awe of what God had done. Assenting to the reality that Joseph did believe Mary leads us to trust that Joseph was in awe of the power of God. He was in awe of the child within Mary. He was in awe of her trust in God.

Notice that in Joseph's heart there is no "noise." There is preoccupation of "me." To be in awe requires being in the presence of something bigger than me. Here, I am confronted with a question: "Do *I* really believe *that* that kind of holiness is possible?" When I consider that Joseph, who was "just like me," was capable of having a heart like this, I am stunned and ask myself: Could that be possible for me? It is then that I beg God to help me as he helped Joseph. It is then that I long for more.

What about you? Do you believe more is possible? What do you want from God? What do you *really* want from God?

For Your Prayer

Today read Romans, chapter 12. Read it a few times. What is God saying to you in the Bible passage? How does it apply to your life? What do you want to say to God?

"Father, I beg you to raise my standards. Transform my mind and the way I think so that I can believe in what you desire for me."

What words stood out to you as you prayed?
What did you find stirring in your heart?

_____
_____
_____
_____
_____
_____
_____
_____
_____
_____
_____
_____
_____
_____
_____
_____
_____
_____
_____
_____
_____

HUMILITY

" Such knowledge is
too wonderful for
me; it is high,
I cannot attain it. **"**

—Psalm 139:6

TODAY IS AN

important day. Therefore, as one who is walking with you, I ask for your patience and time. I invite you to go deeper today. Without a doubt, today's meditation on Matthew 1:19 remains *the* Scripture passage that will help us understand the depth of Joseph's heart, while challenging our historical understanding of the Advent story. Matthew 1:18-19 reads: "When his mother Mary had been betrothed to Joseph, before they came together she was found to be with child of the Holy Spirit; and her husband Joseph, being a just man and unwilling to put her to shame, resolved to send her away quietly."[12] *Why* did Joseph resolve "to send her away quietly"?

This explanation might help us:

> Catholic tradition proposes three main interpretations to explain why Joseph resolved to end his betrothal with Mary.
>
> • *The Suspicion Theory.* Some hold that Joseph suspected Mary of adultery when he discovered her pregnancy. Joseph thus intended to pursue a divorce in accord with Deuteronomy 24:1-4 until the angel revealed to him the miraculous cause of the conception …
>
> • *The Perplexity Theory.* Others hold that Joseph found the situation of Mary's pregnancy inexplicable. Divorce seemed to be his only option, and yet he wished to do this quietly, for he could not bring himself to believe that Mary had been unfaithful …

- *The Reverence Theory*. Still, others hold that Joseph knew the miraculous cause of Mary's pregnancy from the beginning, i.e., he was made aware that the child was conceived 'of the Holy Spirit' ... Faced with this, Joseph considered himself unworthy to be involved in the Lord's work, and his decision to separate quietly from Mary was a discretionary measure to keep secret the mystery within her. On this reading, the angel confirms what Joseph had already known and urges him to set aside pious fears that would lead him away from his vocation to be the legal father of the Messiah ... Joseph is said to be righteous because of his deep humility and reverence for the miraculous works of God. Proponents of this view include St. Bernard of Clairvaux and St. Thomas Aquinas."[13]

St. Bernard of Clairvaux and St. Thomas Aquinas invite us to consider the "Reverence Theory" mentioned above. Perhaps Joseph's choosing to "send her away quietly" was not because he did not understand that Mary's conception was through the Holy Spirit but rather because he *did* understand. Let's consider this.

The Old Testament Ark of the Covenant was the sacred vessel God prepared for the Ten Commandments (see Exodus 25:10-22). It was the sacred vessel that contained the words of God. The Ark of the Covenant was so sacred that in 2 Samuel we read how Uzzah died immediately after touching the ark because he himself was unclean (see 2 Samuel 6:1-7). Astonished, King David exclaimed, "How can the ark of the Lord come to me?" (2 Samuel 6:9).

As a just man, Joseph would have been steeped in the truths of the Old Testament, and, therefore, Joseph would have been very familiar with Uzzah's death. Even more sacred than the Old Testament vessel that contained the words of God, Mary is the new vessel that is holding *the* Word made flesh. Mary is the New Ark of the New Covenant, and perhaps Joseph knew it. Perhaps Joseph's decision to divorce her, and to do so quietly, is because he felt unworthy of such a blessing in his life. Perhaps, Joseph was overwhelmed with *humility*. Joseph felt unworthy because Joseph was a man of profound humility.

St. Bernard of Clairvaux defines humility as: "A virtue by which a man knowing himself *as he truly is*, abases himself." [14] Joseph knew himself as he truly was. Who is worthy of receiving the New Ark of the New Covenant into his home? *No one.* Who is holy enough to represent fatherhood to Jesus on behalf of God the Father? *No one.* Who is worthy of receiving the New Eve into his own marriage? *No one.* Joseph knows himself as he truly is. He does not pretend to be who he is not. It is Joseph's humility and reverence that leads to his decision.

As we move together through Joseph's heart, I invite you to "feel" what you feel in *his* heart. In Joseph's heart, there is no need to be anyone other than who he is. There is no hum of anxiety. There is no comparison. There is no preoccupation of "me." True humility is knowing who you are. As we shared last Saturday, Joseph knew *who* he was because Joseph knew *whose* he was. Humility is knowing *who* you are because you know *whose* you are. True humility relieves us of the exhausting treadmill of trying to "be" somebody or holding on to who we once were. As you "feel" Joseph's heart do you "feel" the peace? Too many of us spend too much energy trying to "be" somebody for others or we try to hold on to the way we used to look or what we used to be able to do. True humility is knowing who you are.

Joseph's heart shines light on your heart. What about you? *Who* are you? More importantly, *whose* are you?

For Your Prayer

Joseph prayed with the Psalms. Begin by slowly reading Psalm 139:1–16. Read it a few times. Consider how often Joseph prayed with these Old Testament verses. What is God saying to you in the Bible passage? How does it apply to your life? What do you want to say to God?

"Father, I ask for the grace today to know personally your love for me. Help me understand the reality of who I am by further experiencing whose I am."

What words stood out to you as you prayed?
What did you find stirring in your heart?

_____

_____

_____

_____

_____

_____

_____

_____

_____

_____

_____

_____

_____

_____

_____

_____

_____

_____

_____

_____

WORTHY

"

Fear not, for I am with you.

—Isaiah 43:5

"

JOSEPH FELT

unworthy, thus he planned to divorce Mary quietly. Soon, God intervened before Joseph can do any such thing. Matthew 1:20 reads, "But as he considered this, behold, an angel of the Lord appeared to him in a dream, saying, 'Joseph, son of David, do not fear to take Mary your wife, for that which is conceived in her is of the Holy Spirit'" (Matthew 1:20). God intervened. Joseph felt unworthy, and God replied: "Do not fear."

Joseph felt unworthy because *he was*. Who is worthy of receiving the New Ark of the New Covenant into his home? Who is holy enough to represent fatherhood to Jesus on behalf of God the Father? Who is worthy of receiving the New Eve into his own marriage? Joseph felt unworthy because he *was* unworthy. However, God, in a sense, said, "Do not be afraid—I am worthy, and I will be with you."

When we feel unworthy, we often fear that our deepest fear is true: that we are not "good enough" and God will abandon us. Many of us distance ourselves from God—we abandon God before he can abandon us. God knew exactly how Joseph felt and said, "Do not be afraid." Likewise, when you and I feel unworthy, God pursues us with the truth and speaks the same words: "Do not be afraid."

You and I are not worthy. This is actually good news! You are *not* worthy—and you *never will be*. Our worth in life has nothing to do with us and everything to do with God. Regardless of your past— God is with you there. Regardless of your present, and whether or not your life has lived up to your plans—God is with you there. Regardless of mistakes, sinfulness, or patterns of distance—God is with you here.

In Joseph's heart, notice that there is no fear of facing God's truth. In Joseph's heart, there is no fear of "what if God finds out?" *This is freedom.* Even in feeling unworthy, Joseph stands still and allows God to speak to him. Can you "feel" Joseph standing still as he feels unworthy? Can you "feel" what is it like for him to stand still so that God can speak truth to him?

Today, carve out some time for silence. Revisit the questions from yesterday, such as: *Who* are you? More importantly, *whose* are you? Ask God, "Why is it that you choose to love me?" Ask the Lord, "Where does my worth come from?"

For Your Prayer

Joseph prayed with the Old Testament, especially the words from the prophet Isaiah. Begin your prayer by slowly rereading Isaiah 43:1–7. Then, read Isaiah 49:14-16. Read it a few times. Consider how often Joseph prayed with these Old Testament verses. What is God saying to you in the Bible passage? How does it apply to your life? What do you want to say to God?

"Father, I ask for the grace today to know personally your love for me. Help me understand the truth of who I am and the truth of what makes me worthy."

What words stood out to you as you prayed?
What did you find stirring in your heart?

_____
_____
_____
_____
_____
_____
_____
_____
_____
_____
_____
_____
_____
_____
_____
_____
_____
_____
_____
_____

TRUST

" Commit your
way to the Lord;
trust in him,
and he will act. "

—Psalm 37:5

"WHEN JOSEPH WOKE

from sleep, he did as the angel of the Lord commanded him" (Matthew 1:24).

Matthew chapter 1 paints the picture of a man of profound holiness, not a man needing to be convinced regarding divorce. Joseph immediately assented to the angel's message. There is no wavering. There is no reconsideration. There is no asking himself: "What does this mean if I say 'yes'?" Joseph knew who he was because he knew *whose* he was. Joseph *trusts* the One who spoke to him.

There is a difference between trusting *what* a person tells us and trusting the *person* who does the telling. There is a difference between trusting the *plan* and trusting the *voice* of the one who speaks. Joseph knows the One who speaks; Joseph knows God. Once Joseph is clear on who is speaking, everything following is received with surrender. Joseph trusts God, and that is enough.

Sometimes, it is easy when God asks us to trust him. In those moments we can trust the *what* that it makes it easy to trust the *who* is doing the asking. However, on other occasions, it can be more difficult to trust God. Sometimes what God asks of us feels like too much. Or we may feel trapped in the circumstances, and in those moments, we struggle to trust God

One of the more legendary men I have ever met was a pillar of the community at St. Luke's Catholic Church in Thibodaux. Charlie Mack, may he rest in peace, was a man of great wisdom, seasoned by the suffering of life. Charles once said to me: "Life is a lot less about what you're *facing* and a lot more about where you're looking." That is wisdom. Regardless of what we are facing in life, it remains essential that we are always *looking* at the Lord who loves us. Charlie Mack knew that, and Joseph knew that.

In Joseph's heart he deeply believes: "If God said He will do it, it will happen." Even in not knowing "how" Joseph trusts the voice of the One who spoke to him.

Notice today the immediacy of Joseph's trust in God's voice. Where in your life is God asking you to trust him? Have you ever sensed God's invitation to follow him, only to hesitate because of what God was asking? Imagine if you heard God's voice as Joseph did. Imagine if you trusted God as Joseph did. Again today, God is asking you: What do you want from him?

For Your Prayer

Joseph prayed with the Psalms. Begin by slowly reading Psalm 37:1-7. Read it a few times. Consider how often Joseph prayed with these Old Testament verses. What is God saying to you in the Bible passage? How does it apply to your life? What do you want to say to God?

"Father, I ask for the grace today to know personally your love for me. Help me to trust you regardless of what I am facing in life."

What words stood out to you as you prayed?
What did you find stirring in your heart?

_____

_____

_____

_____

_____

_____

_____

_____

_____

_____

_____

_____

_____

_____

_____

_____

_____

_____

_____

_____

Second Week — THURSDAY

RECEIVE

"How can a young
man keep
his way pure?
By guarding
it according to
your word."

—Psalm 119:9

TODAY'S MEDIATION

made more of an impact on me can any of the others. I ask for your patience as I invite you to go deeper today. "When Joseph woke from sleep, he did as the angel of the Lord commanded him; he *took* his wife" (Matthew 1:24, emphasis added). What does this mean? If we are to look at Advent *through the eyes of Joseph*, it is important for us to make a precise biblical distinction here. In the original Greek, the word translated as "took" is *paralambanō*, which literally means "to enter into a close relationship." Where else do we see a similar phrase or at least a reference that can help us appreciate Joseph's virtue? In John 19:26-27, we hear Jesus, on the Cross, speaking to John and Mary: "When Jesus saw his mother, and the disciple whom he loved standing near, he said to his mother, 'Woman, behold, your son.' Then he said to the disciple, 'Behold, your mother.' And from that hour the disciple *took* her to his own home." The same Greek root word translated as "took" is used—*lambanō*, "to enter into a close relationship." (*Paralambanō*, used in Matthew 1:24, is simply an emphatic form of *lambanō*, used in John 19:27.)

Both Joseph and John *receive* Mary. Joseph does not "take" Mary as "his," strictly speaking. Nor does the apostle John "take" Mary as "his." Both men of great virtue *receive* Mary on *her* terms, not theirs. Joseph, much like John, receives Mary "to enter into a close relationship" with her. Joseph saw Mary in such a way that he could receive her.

There are four relational dimensions of mature, integrated manhood: son, brother, husband, and father. Mature, integrated men have a healthy understanding of who they are as sons. The evidence that a man is healthy in his identity as a son is that he does not have the need to compete or prove himself. Next, men learn how to be a brother. Here, men learn how to *see* women for who they are, as sisters, not objects. The evidence that a man is healthy in his identity as a brother is that he *sees* women as they are, not as his imagination compartmentalizes them to be. Only when a man is a healthy son and brother can he be a healthy husband and father. His maturity as a husband is revealed in his purity of *seeing his wife as she is* and, therefore, receiving her and letting her reveal herself to him.

The purity of how Joseph *sees* Mary leads to the purity of how Joseph *receives* Mary. Thus, there is a purity of how Joseph enters into "a close relationship" (*paralambanō*) with her. Their relationship would have been one of profound intimacy, vulnerability, and receptivity precisely because of Mary's sinlessness and Joseph's virtue. Joseph never "takes" from Mary; he always and only *receives* her. For those who may struggle to understand Joseph's marriage to Mary, imagine for a moment what it would be like for a woman of Mary's purity to invite you into her heart, only to expect that same depth of purity from you once you were there. Precisely because of just how close their "close relationship" was, there was nowhere for Joseph to hide. Joseph was forever pierced by purity, with his only posture to *receive* Mary as she was.

In Joseph's heart, notice what we do not notice: there is no fear of being seen as he is. There is no fear of being known by Mary. There is no need to hide from Mary. Joseph is at peace. Can you feel Joseph's docility? Can you feel Joseph's *reverence* for Mary?

There is a difference between thinking *about* God and talking *with* God. How many times must have Joseph had to *turn towards* the Father and share his heart *with* him. After all, loving Mary with the level of purity that she deserved must have taken all that Joseph could offer. Today, be not afraid. Talk with God. Listen to his voice. Trust that God is *receiving* you and your heart.

For Your Prayer

Joseph prayed with the Psalms. Begin by slowly reading Psalm 119:1–16. Read it a few times. Consider how often Joseph prayed with these Old Testament verses. What is God saying to you in the Bible passage? How does it apply to your life? What do you want to say to God?

"*Father, I beg you to pierce my heart with purity. Help me to see others as you see them. Help me to receive others as you receive them.*"

What words stood out to you as you prayed?
What did you find stirring in your heart?

_____

_____

_____

_____

_____

_____

_____

_____

_____

_____

_____

_____

_____

_____

_____

_____

_____

_____

_____

_____

_____

RECEIVE

"With my whole
heart I seek you;
let me not wander
from your
commandments!"

—**Psalm 119:10**

PULL

"We are his workmanship."

—Ephesians 2:10

IN MATTHEW 1:25,

we read, "[Joseph] knew her not *until* she had borne a son; and he called his name Jesus." What does "until" mean here? The Greek term translated as "until" is *heos*, which does *not* imply that Joseph and Mary had marital relations after Jesus' birth. Some infer from this passage that once Jesus' was born, Joseph and Mary then had marital relations. The actual Greek word *heos* does not imply this; the problem here is in the English translation. *Heos* simply indicates a certain period of time, without implying change in the future. Matthew is simply emphasizing that Joseph had no involvement in Mary's pregnancy before Jesus' birth.

Msgr. John Cihak begins to draw us into this mystery: "In marriage, a man's wife changes him. He practices giving himself in love to her. He allows himself to be determined by her. He must attune himself to her, and she engages his heart and helps to develop his *eros* into *agape* love."[15] Most men must learn this. There is greatness inside of every man, but for many men, *this must be pulled out of him*. The love that a husband has for his wife pulls the deepest desires out of him, as he longs "to do mighty deeds for her."[16]

Imagine for a moment what it would be like for a woman of Mary's purity to invite you into her heart, only to expect that same depth of purity from you once you were there. Mary's purity and holiness would have *pulled* the same purity and holiness out of Joseph. Precisely because of just how *close* their "close relationship" was, there was nowhere for Joseph to hide. Mary's holiness meant that Joseph himself had to rise to the occasion and love her with the heroic virtue.

It has been said that when Jesus first saw Simon, he saw "Peter" (i.e., the "Rock") inside of him. Therein, Jesus *pulled* Peter out of Simon. It has been said that when Jesus first saw Simon the fisherman, he saw the Peter the pope inside the fisherman. Therein, Jesus *pulled* the pope out the fisherman. During each stage of life, Jesus seeks to *pull* something out of us. Precisely through the purity of Mary's marriage to Joseph did she *pull* the greatness out of her husband. Her holiness could not do anything but pull the holiness out of Joseph.

There is a Peter inside every Simon. There is a saint inside every sinner. There is greatness inside of *you*. The question is: Will you let God *pull* the saint out the sinner? Will you let God *pull* the greatness out of you?

For Your Prayer

Today read Ephesians 3:14–21. Read it a few times. What is God saying to you in the Bible passage? How does it apply to your life? What do you want to say to God?

"Father, I beg you to make this Advent my best ever. Pull the saint out of this sinner. I give you permission to do far more in me than all than I could ever ask or imagine."

What words stood out to you as you prayed?
What did you find stirring in your heart?

_____

_____

_____

_____

_____

_____

_____

_____

_____

_____

_____

_____

_____

_____

_____

_____

_____

_____

_____

_____

Second Week — SATURDAY

The Third Week of Advent

Journey

THE GOSPEL OF

Luke first mentions Joseph in chapter 2: "In those days a decree went out from Caesar Augustus that all the world should be enrolled. This was the first enrollment, when Quirinius was governor of Syria. And all went to be enrolled, each to his own city. And Joseph also went up from Galilee, from the city of Nazareth, to Judea, to the city of David, which is called Bethlehem, because he was of the house and lineage of David" (Luke 2:1–4).

The population census was called for purposes of determining and collecting taxes. This is what prompted Joseph to leave Nazareth and journey to Bethlehem. Jewish custom required families to be enlisted in their ancestral hometowns, which meant Joseph had to lead his eight-and-a-half-month pregnant wife on a ninety-mile pilgrimage to the city of his ancestors, Bethlehem.

Two thousand years ago, walking was a normal part of life. Considering the quality of their health, most Jewish adults would have easily been able to walk fifteen miles a day. Thus, the ninety-mile journey should have only taken about six days. All of that changed for a pregnant woman. As her pregnancy advanced, Mary's body had less energy. Furthermore, traveling, whether she walked or rode on a donkey, would have created disproportionate pressure on the pelvic area creating lower back discomfort. Without proper support for her lower back, the constant movement in her torso further intensified her aforementioned discomfort. So, their journey would probably have been lengthened to two weeks.

All of Israel was affected by the census. So, Joseph and Mary were not the only ones on pilgrimage. Everyone was talking about the census, either because they themselves had to travel or because they would see their relatives who would travel to visit. As Joseph prepared to travel, he could not help but remember the Old Testament prophecy that the Messiah would be born in Bethlehem, not Nazareth. Joseph understood how the census was actually serving God's plan for humanity. Therefore, the journey to Bethlehem was more than just a journey ninety miles south, it was journey scripted in the heart of God.

Welcome to the third week of Advent. *Welcome to the journey to Bethlehem.*

For Your Prayer

"For our light and momentary troubles are achieving for us an eternal glory that far outweighs them all."
– 2 Corinthians 4:17

RESPONSIBLE

"Unless the Lord

builds the house,

those who build it

labor in vain."

—Psalm 127:1

THE CENSUS WAS

not in Joseph's plans. He had spent the past months getting the home ready for Mary's arrival. He felt *responsible* for providing a home. Furthermore, Joseph felt what every first-time father feels. Of course, the man asks: "Is the baby OK? Is everything going to go as planned during the delivery?" But they also ask: "What are we going to do after? Do we have enough to make it as a family? Can I do this?" When these questions loom deep within a man's heart, it is then that men feel the "burden" of responsibility.

Here comes the census. Joseph must stop everything he was doing to lead his wife and child ninety-miles south. The census caused havoc within the Jewish community, as everyone was on the road to their ancestral hometowns. This meant there was going to be a increased danger in travel. Joseph would have felt the burden of responsibility for protecting his family. Furthermore, they know Mary is due soon, but when? There were no doctors. There was no due date. Joseph feels *responsible* for getting to Bethlehem in time so that Mary can deliver in ease and comfort.

How would you feel if you had to protect the Savior of the world and the only sinless woman born outside the Garden of Eden? How would you feel if you had to lead your eight-and-a-half-month pregnant wife on a two-week journey and every morning you wake up wondering: "Is it today? Is she going to deliver today? Are we going to make it?"

Joseph knew where to go with his heart. God would have continuously reminded him of the difference between *stewardship* and *ownership*, and therein lies the lie of the weight of responsibility. When I own something, it is mine. I have the right to do with it as I desire. On the other hand, it is very different when

I am *entrusted* with something. For example, if I handed you an empty sacred chalice, and asked you to hold it, would you not hold it with reverence? If I handed you a sacred chalice filled with the Precious Blood of Christ, would you not hold it with even more reverence? If I entrust you with something sacred, I am ultimately responsible for guiding you. We are responsible for doing what we have been told, but the owner is responsible for instructing us.

Joseph felt responsible because he was responsible. However, he was responsible as one who was *entrusted* with that which *belonged to God*. Joseph was responsible for *listening to God*—and God was responsible for *everything else*. What about you? Where do you feel responsible? More importantly, where do you "go" with that feeling?

For Your Prayer

Joseph prayed with the Psalms. Begin by slowly reading Psalm 127. Read it a few times. Consider how often Joseph prayed with these Old Testament verses. What is God saying to you in the Bible passage? How does it apply to your life? What do you want to say to God?

"Father, I beg you that I may never confuse stewardship with ownership. Help me trust you with everything. Help me to trust that you are actively involved in my life."

What words stood out to you as you prayed?
What did you find stirring in your heart?

_____

_____

_____

_____

_____

_____

_____

_____

_____

_____

_____

_____

_____

_____

_____

_____

_____

_____

_____

_____

_____

Third Week — SUNDAY

PROVISION

"Incline your ear, and come to me; hear, that **your soul may live**."

—Isaiah 55:3

AS JOSEPH AND

Mary left Nazareth for Bethlehem, Joseph knew where he was going. Old Testament prescriptions required Jewish citizens to make a pilgrimage to Jerusalem three times per year. Joseph knew the roads to Jerusalem well. From the gates of Jerusalem, it was less than ten miles to Bethlehem. Therefore, even if Joseph had never been to Bethlehem, it would not have been difficult to figure out how to get there.

In a certain sense, Joseph knew where he was going. On the other hand, Joseph had never been there before. He had never accompanied his wife, who was nearly ready to give birth, on roads that also had thieves seeking to capitalize on the number of pilgrims. He had never had to predict if he would make it to Bethlehem in time for the birth. He had never prepared to raise the Savior of the world. Could Mary's body handle the journey? Where would they stay once they arrived? Would his meager savings be enough for the census tax plus the journey there and back? Nazareth was already a tiny village with a small economy, to say the least. Furthermore, his work as a carpenter would not have provided a lifestyle of any excess. The journey to Bethlehem would have stretched Joseph's meager means of *provision.*

It is one thing to trust that God will provide. Until God actually comes through, however, it is natural to struggle with anxiety. In those moments, when fear nipped at Joseph, his knowledge of Scripture was his comfort. Joseph recalled Abraham, and God's providing him a son, Moses' way through the Red Sea, and Elijah's food under the broom tree. When Joseph struggled with trusting God's provision, the Scriptures were the balm for Joseph's anxiety. When Joseph worried about provision he would go to the Scriptures.

Many men know the *burden* of provision. At the end of the day, when all are resting in bed, many men know what it is like to lie awake worrying about the souls in those beds, the finances needed to provide for their sustenance, and a myriad of other things regarding provision. The hidden trap of worrying about provision is not as much the anxiety as it is the interior isolation. Many men retreat to their heads, isolating themselves by trying to figure out what to do and how to fix their situations on their own. Thus, they may feel as if all of the pressure is on them.

The question is not if you feel anxiety regarding provision; the question is *where do you go* with this anxiety? What is in your heart these days regarding provision? More importantly, where are you going with any anxiety?

For Your Prayer

Joseph prayed with the Old Testament, especially the words from the prophet Isaiah. Begin your prayer by slowly rereading Isaiah, chapter 55. Read it a few times. Consider how often Joseph prayed with these Old Testament verses. What is God saying to you in the Bible passage? How does it apply to your life? What do you want to say to God?

"Father, I beg you to help me trust you. Help me trust you with everything. Help me to trust that you are actively involved in my life."

What words stood out to you as you prayed?
What did you find stirring in your heart?

_____

_____

_____

_____

_____

_____

_____

_____

_____

_____

_____

_____

_____

_____

_____

_____

_____

_____

_____

_____

Third Week — MONDAY

COMPARISON

> " I lift up my
> eyes to the hills.
> From whence does
> my help come?
> My help comes
> from the Lord,
> who made heaven
> and earth. "

—Psalm 121:1-2

AS MENTIONED

in this week's introduction, all of Israel was affected by the census. Jewish custom required families to be enlisted in their ancestral hometowns. Therefore, Joseph and Mary were not the only ones on pilgrimage. Imagine the scene. There were thousands walking to the hometowns of their ancestors. Joseph set a pace that honored Mary's pregnancy. Going much slower than other families occupying the road, faster pilgrims traveling north to south were constantly passing Joseph from behind. With each pass, Joseph and Mary shared "hellos" and courteous greetings. As the passing family slowly moved out of sight, Joseph's eyes could not help but notice their provisions compared to the meager reserve in his possession. The same was true for those who traveled south to north. They occupied the other side of the road. Joseph could see them coming toward him. As he anticipated the same "hellos" and courteous greetings, he also could not help but notice what they had in *comparison* to what he had.

With each pass, there was the natural glance at the pilgrims and their provisions. Each glance gave rise to a new *comparison*, as Joseph looked at his situation in light of their situation. In those moments when the whispers of *comparison* nipped at Joseph's interior peace, we can imagine Joseph turning his gaze from the road to his wife. There, with Mary knowing well what was going on in Joseph's heart, all Joseph needed to do was see the intensity of trust in her eyes. In silence, Mary would gaze at Joseph. Then, in silence with a simple glance to her hands caressing her womb, Mary's eyes said all that Joseph needed to hear. Joseph may not have had what the others had on their pilgrimages, but no one on those roads—or anyone in the world or ever in human history—had what Joseph had on his pilgrimage. In comparison, Joseph had the most treasured gift in all of history, and that suddenly put all his comparison into perspective.

Men often battle the enemy of *comparison*. Many men are tempted to compare their competence at providing. They compare themselves to others, judging what they have against what others have. Of course, the seduction of comparison never reveals the truth. When we compare, we compare what we *actually* have versus what we *assume* others have.

Here is an example. Imagine a fictitious man. Let's call him "Adam." Adam and his family enter church on any random Sunday. As he sits in the pew, he "hears" silence for the first time since he left church the previous Sunday. In the silence, all of the imperfections of his life come to light: his kids arguing on the way to church, his wife's longing for him to lead spiritually, and the hum of anxiety regarding his job, among other things. After sitting in the pew for two minutes, another family enters the church and sits in the pew in front of him. Adam now unknowingly compares his situation to theirs. All he sees is their ironed clothes, courteous "hellos," and well-preserved beauty. Furthermore, as the man in front of him bows his head, Adam presumes in the comparison that the other man is praying with ease. Adam compares his situation to the family in front of him. However, *the seduction of comparison never reveals the truth.* Adam has no idea that the guy in front of him, as soon as he bowed his head, was nipped with thoughts of his own kids arguing on the way to church, his own wife's longing for him to lead spiritually, and the hum of anxiety regarding his own job. Adam compared his life to what he *imagined* the other guy had. Of course, anyone who does this will always lose in the end.

We can compare ourselves to other people—or, worse yet, to the expectations we have of ourselves or feel others have of us. Especially at this time of year, we may be tempted to assess what we are providing by way of presents and material possessions in comparison to what others are providing. We can compare where we are in life to where we thought we would be or where others think we should be. We can compare what did happen to what did not happen, and vice versa. Comparison is a vicious enemy and lures us into a battle that we are destined to lose every time.

Notice that "Adam" is caught within himself, looking at himself. Notice that in comparison you and I are caught within ourselves, looking at ourselves. Remember my good friend Charlie Mack? "Life is a lot less about what you're facing and a lot more about where you're looking." That is never more important than with *comparison*. It is about where you are looking. When we are facing the temptation of comparison, it is important to look to the Lord so that he can put things in perspective. That is what Joseph did. That is what Joseph can teach you.

How are you doing with comparison? When do you compare? When are you most susceptible to comparison? Specifically, at this time of year, what does comparison look like or feel like?

For Your Prayer

Joseph prayed with the Psalms. Begin by slowly reading Psalm 121. Read it a few times. Consider how often Joseph prayed with these Old Testament verses. What is God saying to you in the Bible passage? How does it apply to your life? What do you want to say to God?

"Father, I beg you to help me trust you. Help me trust you with everything. Help me to trust that you are actively involved in my life."

**What words stood out to you as you prayed?
What did you find stirring in your heart?**

_____

_____

_____

_____

_____

_____

_____

_____

_____

_____

_____

_____

_____

_____

_____

_____

_____

_____

_____

_____

_____

_____

_____

Third Week — TUESDAY

PRESENT

"In peace,
I will both lay
down and sleep;
for you alone,
O Lord, make me
dwell in safety."

—Psalm 4:8

IMAGINE THE

scene. The sun was setting, and Joseph had already spotted a place where he and Mary could make camp for the night. As daylight faded, Joseph built a small fire. He instinctively tended to Mary's comfort, asking her how she felt, what she needed, and how he might help her. He then prepared dinner: goat cheese, bread, a few figs, and olives. Before they ate, as with every meal, they paused for an extended, but natural, silence. Then Joseph prayed aloud, thanking the Lord for the day, their safety, and the food that they were to eat.

With the crackle of the fire drawing them into conversation, Joseph and Mary spent the evening in conversation. Joseph asked Mary about her comfort and lower back. Mary asked Joseph about his energy and aching feet. They talked about the people they saw on the day's journey and the conversations they enjoyed with pilgrims who passed them by. As is natural, conversation deepened with each new branch on the fire. Mary mentioned that she felt the child moving in her womb. Joseph wondered aloud asking: "What will he look like? What will he be like?" They each shared their emotions, fears, and dreams. Then, as the fire was waning and the sky was fully alive with stars, Mary sang quietly. The child in her womb knew her voice and would respond every time she sang. Joseph too loved her voice and it served as comfort to his tired body. As his eyes grew heavy, Mary grinned as he fought to stay awake. With tenderness, she gently guided his head to rest on her womb. Singing still, but now with greater tenderness, Mary caressed Joseph's head until he was asleep in seconds. Now, alone in silence, Mary smiled with inexpressible gratitude for the two men God the Father chose just for her: Joseph, the man sent to protect her, and Jesus, the man sent to save her.

Every day, the average American spends nearly four hours looking at their smartphone and another four hours in front of a television. The hours spent with media has nearly doubled in the past twenty years. If I asked someone twenty years ago if they thought they would spend one-third of their day in front of a screen devoid of any human interaction, most people would have called me crazy. However, when we get swept up in the trajectory of the secular culture and cease to discern if where we are heading is healthy, we wind up being somewhere we never thought we would be.

Do you live in the *present moment*? When you do, what is your experience? What prevents you from living in the present moment? What intentional choices do you have to make in order to live *presently* to the present moment?

For Your Prayer

Joseph prayed with the Old Testament, especially the words from the prophet Isaiah. Begin your prayer by slowly reading a single verse from Isaiah, chapter 65. Read Isaiah chapter 65:1. Read it a few times. Consider how many times God was wanted to be with us in the present moment and yet how many times we missed him. What is God saying to you in the Bible verse? How does it apply to your life? What do you want to say to God?

"Father, I beg you to help me live in the present moment. Teach me what changes are needed in my life in order for me to live in the present moment."

What words stood out to you as you prayed?
What did you find stirring in your heart?

_____

_____

_____

_____

_____

_____

_____

_____

_____

_____

_____

_____

_____

_____

_____

_____

_____

_____

_____

_____

_____

SILENCE

" For God alone,
my soul waits
in silence; from
him comes
my salvation. "

—Psalm 62:1

TRIPS LIKE THE

one to Bethlehem are filled with *silence*. In the silence, Joseph relied on the Father's voice. On Sunday, I mentioned that Joseph was responsible as one who was entrusted with that which ultimately belonged to God. That meant Joseph was responsible for *listening to God*, and God was responsible for *everything* else. As Joseph was being led by God, he was *listening* to God.

It is one thing to be led when you can hear God speaking to you. However, when God seems silent, or when we cannot settle or quiet ourselves into listening, being led becomes more difficult. When we cannot hear God's voice, it is hard to see God leading us. When we cannot see God lead, we get restless and soon leave the posture of being led. We are tempted to seize control. That pattern always works for us; however, we then mistake silence for absence and assume that no one is leading.

Sometimes, silence is like a magnet. The silence allows other things to rise to the surface, such as issues embedded deep within our heart. Once those hidden things rise to the surface, then God can speak. Sometimes, God's silence actually "speaks": "*There are other things I want to talk to you about. Now, let me be quiet so those things can come to the surface.*" On the ninety-mile trek to Bethlehem, Joseph certainly would have heard God speak. Likewise, there would have been moments where Joseph would have heard nothing but silence. In those moments, instead of panicking because God was silent, Joseph would have been attentive to the subtle movements of his heart, relating to God all that stirred within. —————————————————————

How are you with silence? Maybe it is easy for you, or maybe it is difficult. Many struggle with silence, especially at this time of year. However, there is no time of year that we most need to hear as much as we do now.

How are you when God gets quiet? Pay attention to any fear, panic, or judgment of what those feelings mean. More importantly, pay attention to what stirs within you when the silence begins to get too "loud." Remember—silence allows issues embedded deep within our heart to rise. Do not be afraid of the silence or the things that surface.

As we get closer to Christmas, we get closer to a person— Jesus. Resist the tidal surge of activity and actually slow down. Carve out more time for him. Carve out more time for silence. There is so much waiting for you.

For Your Prayer

Joseph prayed with the Psalms. Begin by slowly reading Psalm 62. Read it a few times. Consider how often Joseph prayed with these Old Testament verses. What is God saying to you in the Bible passage? How does it apply to your life? What do you want to say to God?

"Father, I beg you to help me slow down. Help me hear you. Help me stay still long enough to let you lead my heart closer to you. In the quiet, if I feel fear, help me to know you are there."

What words stood out to you as you prayed?
What did you find stirring in your heart?

_____

_____

_____

_____

_____

_____

_____

_____

_____

_____

_____

_____

_____

_____

_____

_____

_____

_____

_____

_____

_____

REMEMBER

> "I will call to mind
> the deeds of the
> Lord; yea, I will
> remember thy
> wonders of old."

—Psalm 77:11

WITH NAZARETH

far behind them and Bethlehem in sight, Mary was beginning to indicate that delivery was imminent. She was quiet, drawn into a deep place of contemplation for all that was about to happen. As she considered that soon she would see God's face, touch God's body, and hear God's voice, she also knew well that Joseph had a lot going on inside his heart. With every step closer to Bethlehem, Joseph stepped further into uncertainty and deeper into dependency. He did not know if they would make it to Bethlehem in time. He did not know how to deliver a baby, much less *this* baby. He did not know how to be a father, much less how to raise the Son of God. In the final hours of Joseph's leading Mary to Bethlehem, Joseph certainly felt all the emotions natural to any man in that situation. However, Joseph also kept his heart and mind engaged with the Lord, and it was in those moments that God helped Joseph *remember*.

The thoughts we think and hear when we are in panic and worry are very different from the thoughts we think and hear when we are calm and reserved. Our thoughts often deceive us when we worry because they come more from the panic than they do from the Lord. Therefore, when you cannot trust your thoughts, trust your *memory*.

Memory is an essential part of the spiritual life. I would encourage you to *remember* all that God has done. What were the meditations that most tugged at your heart? What were the Scripture passages that most spoke to you? What have you learned about Joseph? What do you *remember* from the past twenty days?

Within every graced moment of contact with God, we, finite beings, experience the infinite Lord. Imagine that you are standing beneath a waterfall and all you have is an eight-ounce glass. When you extend your glass under the waterfall to catch the water you cannot receive all that the waterfall can offer. Likewise, when we *remember* what God has done, we can return to "the waterfall" to see if there is more water. If you return to some of the more meaningful meditations or prayer experiences from the past twenty days, you will not be able to repeat the experience. However, the Lord may still have more to give you in those passages or memories.

For Your Prayer

Today's prayer will be a little different. Today, I encourage you to review the past twenty days. Look back on your daily notations. What has God said to you? What were the meditations, insights, or prayer experiences that most helped you? What were the themes? What has God done for you? Spend some time today *remembering* all that God has done.

"Father, I beg you to help me slow down. Help me to remember all that you have done for me in the past so that I may rest in confidence in what you can do in the future."

What words stood out to you as you prayed?
What did you find stirring in your heart?

_____

_____

_____

_____

_____

_____

_____

_____

_____

_____

_____

_____

_____

_____

_____

_____

_____

_____

_____

ORDINARY

"Be still,
and know that
I am God."

—Psalm 46:10

AS JOSEPH AND

Mary walked to Bethlehem, most of their day was actually rather *ordinary*. The journey was filled with ordinary experiences: ordinary conversation, ordinary silence, and ordinary aches and pains. Men and women often view the ordinary with a different interior lens. Avoiding unintended stereotypes, the ordinary for many men equates to provision: work, routine, activity. For many men, the ordinary can feel tiresome and draining. Perhaps that is why so many men like to play on the weekends, attending sporting events, or spending time outdoors.

Joseph has much to teach the modern man in regards to the ordinary. Joseph lived *with* God and *in* God. His communion with God kept him from being enslaved to the enticement of self-sufficiency. Joseph found God in the ordinary. Therefore, there was no need to overindulge or escape the ordinary because, after all, what would he be looking to escape?

Most of life is ordinary. Our attitude toward the ordinary is most easily understood precisely at this time of year. There is much that is different during December. Our houses are decorated with lights and garlands. Our tables are adorned with far more food than we could ever consume on our own. Our spending peaks and outpaces our budget for the rest of the year. None of those things are good or bad in and of themselves. They simply *are*.

At some point soon we will eventually pick up the Christmas tree, the lights, and the decorations. Our living rooms will return to what they looked like before. The presents will be opened, and our relationships will return to what they were before they were artificially inflated because of the emotion of gift-giving. Soon, life will return to the ordinary. If we are not intentional, we actually may lose sight of the extraordinary *because* of the extraordinary. In just a few days, *the most extraordinary event in the history of humanity will be before us.*

We may be tempted to become inordinately preoccupied with the extraordinary externals of the secular Christmas season; a preoccupation fueled by *a longing to escape the ordinary.* Then, we may wake up on December 25, and Jesus' birth will feel so very ordinary and almost uneventful. However, if we make a decision now to be intentional about who is coming then we can resist the temptation to lose focus. Perhaps, we may wake up December 25, keenly aware of the reality of our ordinary, and because of *who is with us*, Jesus' birth can transform our ordinary to so much more.

Would you like God to transform your ordinary? What do you want for Christmas? What do you *really* want for Christmas?

For Your Prayer

Let us end where we began. Return to Psalm 46, especially verse 10. Read it a few times. Consider all that has happened in your life since you first prayed with these Old Testament verses. What is God saying to you in the Bible passage? How does it apply to your life? What do you want to say to God?

"Father, I beg you to make this Christmas my best ever. Help me to slow down, embrace the quiet, and to find you with me, no matter where I am."

What words stood out to you as you prayed?
What did you find stirring in your heart?

Bethlehem

SMALL

> "God chose the
>
> lowly things
>
> of the world."

—1 Corinthians 1:28

AT THE TIME OF

the pilgrimage, ancient Bethlehem was well over three thousand feet above sea level. Jerusalem was at 3,800 feet, so the descent into the valleys surrounding the city meant travel to Bethlehem would require yet another ascent up the mountainous landscapes of southern Israel. Imagine for a moment all that was within Joseph as he rested while taking in the view of Bethlehem immediately before him. More than ten days into the journey, he was tired. Perhaps his fatigue was because of the miles of walking and constantly attending to Mary's needs. Perhaps his fatigue was due to the interior energy expended. Joseph knew that Mary's delivery was close ... very close. The depth of intercession and dependence on God was a grace that carried Joseph, but the amount of spiritual activity took its toll on the body. Joseph stopped and beheld Bethlehem, and he was tired.

Enter into the scene now, as if it were the present moment. Imagine Joseph taking one last breath before he and Mary begin ascending the mountain. As he inhales, he glances back to Mary and their eyes lock in communion. Her eyes ... her beauty ... her pure and faithful love ... all of this is what Joseph breathes in. There is more than air in him. It is love for her, and love for the infant in her womb, that draws his glance back to the mountain. Imagine how *small* Joseph feels at this moment. Who is he to be chosen by God? Who is he to be chosen by Mary? Who is he to be leading them when he feels that they should be leading him? With his gaze lifting up the mountain, tears flood his eyes. As he takes one deliberate step at a time, the pressure on his aching feet make him feel all the smaller. He can read the path to get to Bethlehem, but he begins to admit to himself that he does not know where he is going when he gets there. Only a few feet after he put his first foot forward, he stops in silence. He feels so small.

Now, imagine: Mary whispers his name: "Joseph." He turns to her. Their eyes meet again. She smiles. He smiles and looks back to the mountain. Taking one step at a time, he leads his family, through his fatigue, up the rocky path. All he needed was her gaze. All he needed was her voice. It is his love for her that gives him courage when he feels small.

For Your Prayer

Find some time today to be alone. Find a quiet space. Slow down. Settle your heart. Close your eyes and ask the Holy Spirit to inspire your imagination and guide you as you pray. Imagine Joseph, the mountain, and his fatigue. Imagine his pausing to breath, his glancing towards Mary, and his feeling small. Visualize the scene. Be *in* the scene. Be *with* Joseph as if it is happening now, in the present moment.

What words stood out to you as you prayed?
What did you find stirring in your heart?

BACK

"When I am afraid,
I put my *trust in you*."

—Psalm 56:3

HOW MANY OF

us have grown desensitized to the reality of Christmas? I have. Because I have become so familiar with the trees, lights, and decorations, it has become too easy for me to wrap up December 25 and quickly go back to the way life was on December 24. Christmas can too easily feel like a *day* rather than *Person*. Days come and go. Days do not change our lives; *people* change our lives. I cannot treat a *person* like I treat a Christmas tree. When I am entrusted with a real Person on December 25, I wake up on December 26 and realize: "This Person is *still here*. He isn't going anywhere. He needs me. He now requires that I change my life. This Person is not like a present. He is *not going away*."

As Joseph slowly inched into the rising foothills of Bethlehem, he became evermore quiet. Mary, as she knew that she was mere hours away from giving birth to the Savior of the world, she too became more contemplative. The steps ascending to Bethlehem were quiet, for both Mary and Joseph had a lot on their minds. *There was no going back.* Once Mary gave birth to the Christ child, their lives would be changed forever. Mary knew this, and Joseph knew this as well. As he walked forward, his mind beheld the deepening realization that life would *never* be the same again.

Enter into the scene now, as if it were the present moment. Imagine Mary holding her pregnant womb and swaying rhythmically on the donkey. Imagine Joseph, walking quietly before them. Listen to the quiet; the scene is so very quiet. Now, imagine, you are walking next to Joseph. You can feel the gait of his stride; you can hear the intake of his breathing. All of a sudden, he stops walking, as if his mind has just realized something utterly life-changing. He is suspended in insight. He stands still, so very still. Slowly, ever so slowly, he turns to Mary. Their eyes meet once again. She smiles. He gazes. Then, almost as if they finish each other's thoughts, they whisper together: "We can never go back to the way it was."

For Your Prayer

Find some time today to be alone. Find a quiet space. Slow down. Settle your heart. Close your eyes and ask the Holy Spirit to inspire your imagination and guide you as you pray. Imagine Joseph stunned in silence. Imagine his pausing, standing still. Imagine his glancing towards Mary and realizing that their life will never be the same. Visualize the scene. Be *in* the scene. Be *with* Joseph as if it is happening now, in the present moment.

What words stood out to you as you prayed?
What did you find stirring in your heart?

_____

_____

_____

_____

_____

_____

_____

_____

_____

_____

_____

_____

_____

_____

_____

_____

_____

_____

_____

_____

Fourth Week—MEDITATION TWO

NEED

"O God, you are
my God,
I seek you,
my soul
thirsts for you."

—Psalm 63:1

FURTHER ASCENDING

more than half way up the mountain to Bethlehem, Joseph soon came face to face with his powerless need. Joseph lacked the certainty and security that most men seek. The Child's birth was probably only days away, but Joseph did not know that for sure. There was no doctor, no due date, no online calendar marking the nuances of Mary's pregnancy.

Imagine what it is like for a man to lead his wife up a mountain without knowing for sure the exact moment she would need him to provide a place for delivery. Imagine the *need* in Joseph's heart.

With each step Bethlehem was closer, but for some reason that did not bring the certainty you would imagine. There was much unknown. Where would they stay? Would there be a room? Would they make it there in time? Yes, so much was unknown.

Joseph *needed* God, and he knew it. Therein is the grace: Joseph knew this. He did not pretend to not need God. He *embraced* his need. "I need God," a place where so many of us run away from, was the place where Joseph knew God would come through.

Enter into the scene now, as if it were the present moment. Imagine that you are walking next to Joseph. It is so quiet you can almost hear the questions racing through his head. Now, for a moment ask the Lord to "feel" his heart there in that moment. Imagine once more: Joseph stops walking yet again. You can "feel" how his pause is composed. You can "feel" the still inside of him. Joseph looks at you. Then, with reverence, he closes his eyes. He whispers aloud. You lean in to listen. You can barely hear, but you capture his words: "God, I *need* you." Then, after a tender moment of silence, Joseph smiles, looks back at you, and begins to take one step closer to Bethlehem.

For Your Prayer

Find some time today to be alone. Find a quiet space. Slow down. Settle your heart. Close your eyes and ask the Holy Spirit to inspire your imagination and guide you as you pray. Imagine Joseph in his composed pause from walking. Imagine his standing still. Imagine his eyes closed as he whispers: "God, I need you." What do you "feel" in his heart? What do you feel in your heart? Visualize the scene. Be *in* the scene. Be *with* Joseph as if it is happening now, in the present moment.

What words stood out to you as you prayed?
What did you find stirring in your heart?

_____

_____

_____

_____

_____

_____

_____

_____

_____

_____

_____

_____

_____

_____

_____

_____

_____

_____

_____

_____

_____

DISCOURAGING

" There was no
place for them. "

—Luke 2:7

POOR, DEPENDENT,

and exhausted, Joseph and Mary finally arrived in Bethlehem. Imagine Joseph's urgency. Mary's contractions had started. The time had come. Joseph was driven, a man on a mission, as he knew: "We need a room."

Joseph naturally had expectations for what would happen, as he thought: "Surely, someone will provide us space." With certainty that God would provide, Joseph's excitement for the baby propelled him to urgently search for a room.

Once again, stop for a moment. Can you feel Joseph's heart? Can you feel his urgency? Can you feel his utter dependence on God?

Enter into the scene now, as if it were the present moment. Imagine that you are walking with Joseph and this is what you hear: "No." "We can't." "I'm sorry." "There's no room." "You can't stay here." "Sir, please, you'll have to try another place." You can hear the whisper inside Joseph's head: "Another place? There is no other place." Then, there is a long silence. Again, in staggering echo, you hear: "There is no other place."

Imagine how *discouraging* it must have felt for Joseph to hear the voice of "no" when all he desperately wanted to hear was a single "yes." Imagine being Joseph. Imagine being hand-picked by God himself, chosen to protect Mary and the vulnerable child in her womb. Now, at the hour when things feel most fragile, all you hear is "no." All you hear is the voice of *discouragement*.

Remembering what we have learned and experienced this week, imagine Joseph yet again stopping to remain composed. He feels small. He knows he cannot go back. He knows he needs God. With reverence Joseph closes his eyes. He whispers aloud. You can barely hear, but you capture his words: "God, I need you."

You can feel Joseph's trust. Joseph's dependency tempers his disappointment. It is *relationship* that tempers discouragement. There, you have learned much about life, Joseph's life, and *your* life. Discouragement is a part of life. It is not *if* you are discouraged, but *when* you are discouraged. When you are discouraged, tell God you need him. Then, remember who you are talking to. When you are discouraged, it is the person you are addressing, not the words you are using, that give you hope.

For Your Prayer

Find some time today to be alone. Find a quiet space. Slow down. Settle your heart. Close your eyes and ask the Holy Spirit to inspire your imagination and guide you as you pray. Imagine Joseph urgently searching for a room. Imagine the clamoring of noise within him as all he hears is "no." What do you "feel" in his heart? What do you feel in your heart? Now, as with yesterday, imagine his eyes closed as he whispers: "God, I need you." What do you "feel" in his heart? What do you feel in your heart? Visualize the scene. Be *in* the scene. Be *with* Joseph as if it is happening now, in the present moment.

What words stood out to you as you prayed?
What did you find stirring in your heart?

_____

_____

_____

_____

_____

_____

_____

_____

_____

_____

_____

_____

_____

_____

_____

_____

_____

_____

_____

_____

_____

_____

Fourth Week—MEDITATION FOUR

ANOTHER

> **"I will comfort them, and give them gladness for sorrow."**
>
> —Jeremiah 31:13

JOSEPH RETURNED

to Mary and shared with her the news that she suspected: There was no room for them inside Bethlehem. Perhaps the census crowds were merely too much for the ancient city of David. Perhaps the timing of their request was off. Perhaps they could come back tomorrow. Then again, Mary's contractions were quickening. The need was not tomorrow; it was now.

Enter into the scene now, as if it were the present moment. Imagine that you are with Joseph and Mary. Joseph looks at Mary and says: "There is nowhere else I would rather be." Mary looks at Joseph and says: "There is no one else I would rather be with." She smiles. He smiles. Then, after extended gaze, Joseph turns confidently to lead his wife to the outskirts of Bethlehem.

Mary had a way of doing that. Sometimes her smile was all it took. Other times her words would pierce his heart. There was something about the way Mary loved that disarmed all that was within Joseph. Certainly, Joseph needed God, but Joseph needed Mary. Mary needed Joseph. They needed each other. We all need an "other." We all need people in our life who can be the voice of God or his instrument in loving us. You have heard it said: No man is an island. We all need an "other"; we all need *another*. We all need someone in our life we can touch so that God can touch us.

Enter again into the scene, as if it were the present moment. Joseph makes his way to the caves on the outside of the city. At least there he can find shelter, and perhaps even hospitality. As he walks, with his hand on the rope that guides the donkey, Mary senses the return of the whispers of discouragement. Imagine you are there with them. Setting aside her discomfort, she laughs aloud and says to Joseph: "Do you remember the time when …" Before she finishes the sentence, Joseph was already laughing. He volleys back to her: "Do you remember when …" She too laughs. It was precisely what Joseph needed at the moment. But, then again, Mary had a way of knowing what Joseph needed. Joseph needed Mary. Mary needed Joseph. They needed each other. We all need an "other"; we all need *another*.

For Your Prayer

Find some time today to be alone. Find a quiet space. Slow down. Settle your heart. Close your eyes and ask the Holy Spirit to inspire your imagination and guide you as you pray. Imagine the tenderness of how Joseph looks at Mary. Imagine the way Mary looks at Joseph. Visualize the scene. Be *in* the scene. Be *with* Joseph as if it is happening now, in the present moment. Ask them to show you how they needed each other.

What words stood out to you as you prayed?
What did you find stirring in your heart?

_____

_____

_____

_____

_____

_____

_____

_____

_____

_____

_____

_____

_____

_____

_____

_____

_____

_____

_____

Fourth Week—MEDITATION FIVE

FIND

"Did I not tell you that if you believed, you would see the glory of God?"

—John 11:40

THE MOST TRUSTED

biblical tradition places the birth of Jesus outside of Bethlehem. The mountains were littered with hundreds of caves, and many of them had been used as stables since ancient times. Some of the caves were used by shepherds. After walking with his flock during the day, shepherds would have herded the sheep together by nightfall. The sheep would sleep in the cave, safe from the weather and any predators. Other caves served as homes for families. Depending on the size of the cave and its slope on the mountain, one could either use the cave itself or "build out" on the outside of the entrance.

As Joseph exited the central streets of Bethlehem, he made way for the caves outside the city. It was there that he would find a place for his wife and the Savior of the world. As Joseph found the cave, perhaps it was God who found him. Because Joseph stayed engaged in relationship with God, the voices of discouragement did not win. Joseph stayed still enough to let God find him.

Fr. Larry Gillick, S.J. is a spiritual director filled with wisdom. Perhaps his spiritual sight is heightened by his physical blindness. He tells the story of one day getting lost while walking through town. Unable to see, he panicked and began to pray. The Lord responded to his plea, "Sit in the middle of the street." Puzzled, Fr. Larry questioned, and soon God replied, "Put yourself in a position to be found." A car driven by one of Fr. Larry's friends drove up soon after. Fr. Larry found himself safe and sound, resting on keen spiritual wisdom—when we are lost and cannot see our way out, stop trying to guide yourself ... simply *put yourself in a position to be found.*

Enter into the scene now, as if it were the present moment. Imagine that you are right there on the side of Joseph as he is walking. As he walks, he prays. Instead of trying to find a place, Joseph is trying to find a voice—the voice of God. Joseph knows that at this very moment God is trying to find him as much as Joseph is trying to find a place. Interiorly, even with all that is going on within, Joseph is anchored enough to *put himself in a position to be found.*

For Your Prayer

Find some time today to be alone. Find a quiet space. Slow down. Settle your heart. Close your eyes and ask the Holy Spirit to inspire your imagination and guide you as you pray. Imagine the dependence of Joseph on God. In the intensity of all that was, what does Joseph do to interiorly "stay still" so that he can hear God speaking to him. Visualize the scene. Be *in* the scene. Be *with* Joseph as if it is happening now, in the present moment. Ask them to show you how they needed each other.

What words stood out to you as you prayed?
What did you find stirring in your heart?

_____

_____

_____

_____

_____

_____

_____

_____

_____

_____

_____

_____

_____

_____

_____

_____

_____

_____

_____

_____

WAIT

"Be still before the
Lord, and wait
patiently for him."

—Psalm 37:7

TODAY, LET US

enter into the scene as if it were the present moment. Imagine that you are *there*. *You* are *there*. Walking right at the side of Joseph, he takes notice of a cave. A poor, simple, yet generous couple lives there. Joseph steps forward to speak to the husband on behalf of his family. As his eyes lock with the man who occupies the cave, the woman runs to Mary noticing her labor. There are no words between the men. The man who occupies the cave knows how he would feel if he were in Joseph's shoes. Immediately, he acquiesces and invites Joseph and Mary to the back of the house, in the cave, where the animals are.

You are *there*. Joseph escorts the donkey into the cave. Then, Joseph with tenderness and strength gently guides Mary down to the earth. The cave is safe and dry, but it is poor and meager. It is hardly what one would expect for the God of the universe and the Word made flesh. You can feel the damp, cool, earthen floor. In fact, just when you least expect it, Joseph swiftly turns to you and ask *you* to help.

You are *there*. You can feel the cave's dirt floor pressing against your knees as you kneel down to help.

It is time.

Now.

It has come to *this* moment. Mary and Joseph are now mere seconds away from the birth of the Savior. You look to the left and to the right and see that even the manger's animals are attentive in intrigue. The time has come.

Mary's labor intensifies. Joseph clutches her hand. Mary grabs yours for support. Heaven lunges forward. With Mary's soul singing her refrain of praise she gasps for one last breath. Your eyes widen; your heart quickens. The baby is seconds away ...

For Your Prayer

Find some time today to be alone. Find a quiet space. Slow down. Settle your heart. Close your eyes and ask the Holy Spirit to inspire your imagination and guide you as you pray. Imagine Joseph stunned in silence. Imagine his pausing, standing still. Imagine his glancing towards Mary and realizing that life will never be the same. Visualize the scene. Be *in* the scene. Be *with* Joseph as if it is happening now, in the present moment.

What words stood out to you as you prayed?
What did you find stirring in your heart?

_____

_____

_____

_____

_____

_____

_____

_____

_____

_____

_____

_____

_____

_____

_____

_____

_____

_____

_____

_____

_____

SEE

"Come and

see *what God*

has done!"

—Psalm 66:5

IT IS QUIET; IT IS

still. In the quiet caves outside Bethlehem, Mary and Joseph are mere seconds away from the birth of the Savior. With the manger's animals attentive in intrigue, the time comes. Mary's labor intensifies. Joseph clutches her hand. Heaven lunges forward. With Mary's soul singing her refrain of praise, she gasps for one last breath. Your eyes widen; your heart quickens. The baby is seconds away …. and … finally … he is here … the long-awaited Messiah has been born! Imagine the scene. Joseph gently receives the newborn infant from Mary's womb and instinctively rests Jesus on Mary's chest. As Mary embraces this tiny child, she is captured with a gaze that only mothers can describe. Yet, with all her emotion brimming, she is stunned with inexpressible adoration, for Mary is beholding God himself. Mary is gazing at her son. Mary is gazing at *God*.

Billions of people had been born before Jesus' birth, and none of them saw God face to face. There were three hundred million people alive at the time of Jesus' birth, and none of them were chosen for this moment. This is not merely a baby, *this is God*. God is *not* invisible. God has a face; God has a name. We can see God in our midst. As Mary embraces her son, she is stunned that the almighty God is merely six inches away from her eyes.

Many of us struggle to *see* God. In the busyness of the Christmas holiday rush it is often difficult to *see* God. Even in the joy of presents, family dinners and Christmas carols, it can be difficult to see God. When life fails to meet our expectations, it can be difficult to see God. When life is hard, and the road is tough it can be difficult to see God.

To you I say: "Merry Christmas" you *can* now *see* God. God is not invisible. He is not hidden. Emmanuel, *God is with us*, reminds us all that God wants us to see him in our life. Today will be busy; today will be full. In the midst of it all ask Jesus to help you see him in the midst of these most sacred of days.

For Your Prayer

The Psalms are the sacred music of a chosen people. The Psalms were written as songs to praise God. Imagine how Mary and Joseph would have sung the Psalms during the most silent of nights outside Bethlehem. Begin by slowly reading Psalm 24:6; Psalm 27:13; Psalm 66:5. Read them a few times. Consider the sweetness of the singing. Now, prayerfully imagine the scene in Luke 2:7. Be *in* the scene. Be *with* Mary and Joseph. Be *with* Joseph as he gently receives the newborn infant from Mary's womb. Be *with* Joseph as he instinctively rests Jesus on Mary's chest. Be *with* Mary as she embraces this tiny newborn. Now, ask Mary if you too can hold the firstborn son. Ask Mary if you can hold Jesus … and remember … you're holding *God*.

"Father, I desire to experience joy in a way I have never experienced before. I give you permission to give me a newfound awe at your birth."

What words stood out to you as you prayed?
What did you find stirring in your heart?

SEE

"Therefore the Lord himself
will give you a sign.
Behold, a virgin shall conceive
and bear a son, and shall
call his name Immanuel."

—Isaiah 7:14

What's

Next?

Gain a **Deeper Understanding** of the **Sacraments**

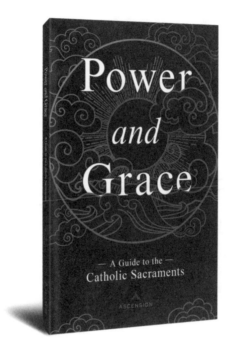

Power and Grace: A Guide to the Catholic Sacraments

by Aimee and Colin MacIver

Have you ever wondered why the sacraments are so important to our Catholic Faith and desired a deeper understanding of these mysteries given to us by God? This beautifully designed, easy-to-read guidebook uncovers the power of these mysteries given to us by God in an engaging and easy-to-understand way. Explanations and discussion questions spark a greater curiosity about the Faith.

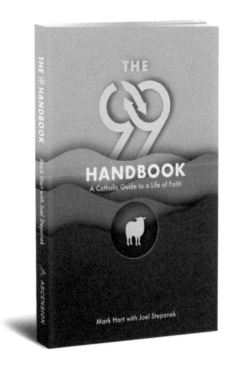

Deepen Your Experience
of Praying the Rosary

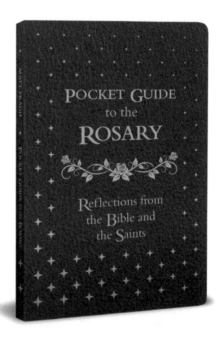

Pocket Guide to the Rosary:
Reflections from the Bible and Saints

by Matt Fradd

The Pocket Guide to the Rosary features insights, Scriptural background, and personal applications for every mystery of the Rosary, so you can focus while in prayer and take advantage of the tremendous graces available to us through the Holy Rosary.

ENDNOTES

1   Pope Benedict XVI, Jesus of Nazareth: *The Infancy Narratives*, 39

2   Ibid.

3   *Redemptoris Custos* 7

4   Ibid, 20

5   Pope Benedict XVI, Church of the Charterhouse of Serra San Bruno, October 9, 2011

6   St. Augustine, *Confessions*

7   *Redemptoris Custos* 18

8   Ibid.

9   St. John Paul II, August 21, 1996

10   St. Thomas Aquinas, *Summa Theologiae* I–II, 26, 4, corp. art.

11   Pope Benedict XVI, *Jesus of Nazareth: The Infancy Narratives*, 39

12   *The Ignatius Catholic Study Bible New Testament*

13   Ibid.

14   See Catholic Encyclopedia, volume 7, pg. 543

15   Msgr. John Cihak, S.T.D. "The Blessed Virgin Mary's Role in the Celibate Priest's Spousal and Paternal Love"

16   Ibid.